P9-DXN-318

The Color Nature Library

THE WONDERS OF NATURE

By
JACQUELINE SEYMOUR

Designed by
DAVID GIBBON

Produced by
TED SMART

CRESCENT BOOKS

INTRODUCTION

Two main sources of energy cause the shaping of the Earth's surface and the alteration of landscapes. Energy derived from the Sun drives the circulation of the atmosphere and supports life, and the Earth's internal heat is responsible for major earth movements and volcanoes; the average annual solar radiation received at the Earth's surface is 4,000 times the average annual heat flow from the interior so solar effects are more important than internal ones. Another force which provides energy is that of gravity; gravitational attraction by the Sun and the Moon is responsible for the tides and the downward pull of the Earth's gravity is a driving force in all forms of erosion.

Even though the energy released from the interior of the Earth is so much less than that received from the Sun the changes which are powered in this way are enormous and are responsible for the major architectural features of the Earth's crust. It has been known since the seventeenth century that the coastlines of Africa and South America are strikingly similar; the fit is so good that the continents could have been joined at some time. This observation led to the formulation of the theory of Continental Drift, which suggests that the continents as we know them have been formed by the break up of a single large land mass and have drifted to their present positions. The more recent Plate Tectonic theory explains how this could have happened. The Earth's crust is very thin, about thirty kilometres in depth, and represents less than one half of one per cent of the radius of the earth. The so-called mantle is the next layer, about 3,000 kilometres thick and the metallic core has a radius of about the same distance. The crust is of two distinct types, continental and oceanic, and consists of six large plates and many smaller ones; all major crustal processes can be related to the relative movements of these plates. As the plates move, virtually floating on the underlying mantle, they can slip past each other, or collide, or pull apart. This is happening extremely slowly, but not so slowly that it cannot be measured. The Mid-Atlantic Ridge is a long submarine mountain range which runs down the middle of the Atlantic from the Arctic to the Antarctic and is located at the junction between two plates. The Ridge breaks the surface in places, forming volcanic islands such as Iceland, the Azores and Tristan da Cunha, and is constantly being added to by the extrusion of molten basaltic rock rising from the mantle as the plates drift apart at an approximate rate of four centimetres a year. All ocean floors are being added to by the extrusion of new rock at undersea ridges; measurements show that the rate of horizontal movement varies from one to ten centimetres a year on each side of a ridge.

Sea floor spreading at one location implies destruction of the oceanic crust at another and this is indeed what is happening. Where two plates meet one is deflected downwards by the other. The plate descending into the mantle carries oceanic crust with it, the surface sediments being deformed in the process producing mountain ranges. The Andes are the result of a collision between an oceanic and a continental plate; the Himalayas arise from a collision between two continental plates; the oceanic crust which is thought to have originally separated these two plates being totally consumed. Sometimes plates slide past each other creating an earthquake zone such as the one associated with the San Andreas fault which results from movement of the Pacific and North American plates.

The present configuration of the Earth's crust is the result of erosion and deposition of eroded sediment as well as of the large-scale movements just described, all these processes going on simultaneously. The first stage in erosion of rock material is weathering, which consists of both mechanical disintegration and chemical breakdown. Mechanical weathering occurs in a number of ways. Rocks at the surface are under less pressure than they were deep down and the release of this pressure and the deformation caused by mountain building usually mean that the surface rocks are thoroughly fractured. The way is therefore open for other processes such as the formation of ice in the fissures or the penetration of tree roots. Chemical breakdown is achieved largely by water which usually has other substances dissolved in it making its action even more potent. Climate obviously plays an important part in weathering; in the humid tropics the effect is different from that in arid zones and from that in cold regions.

Once weathering has occurred transportation of the eroded material can take place. Winds, glaciers and ocean waves all erode and transport material, but all but a small fraction of the rock waste is carried from the land to the sea by rivers. Deposition or sedimentation on the sea bed is the first stage in the formation of new sedimentary rocks which at present make up three-quarters of the exposed rocks of the world.

James Hutton, the eighteenth century Scottish geologist, first recognised the existence of such a ceaseless and self-renewing cycle. He could see within the rocks around him evidence of the same processes that were actually happening at the time, such as erosion, deposition and volcanic activity. His views have been encapsulated in the phrase "The present is the key to the past" and his ideas are generally accepted today. Geomorphological studies are being more intensely pursued now than ever before. The understanding they bring is being put to useful purposes and may even lead to the prevention of some earthquakes in the future.

Left: Earth as seen from Apollo 17 showing an area extending from the Mediterranean to the South Polar icecap with heavy cloud over the southern hemisphere.

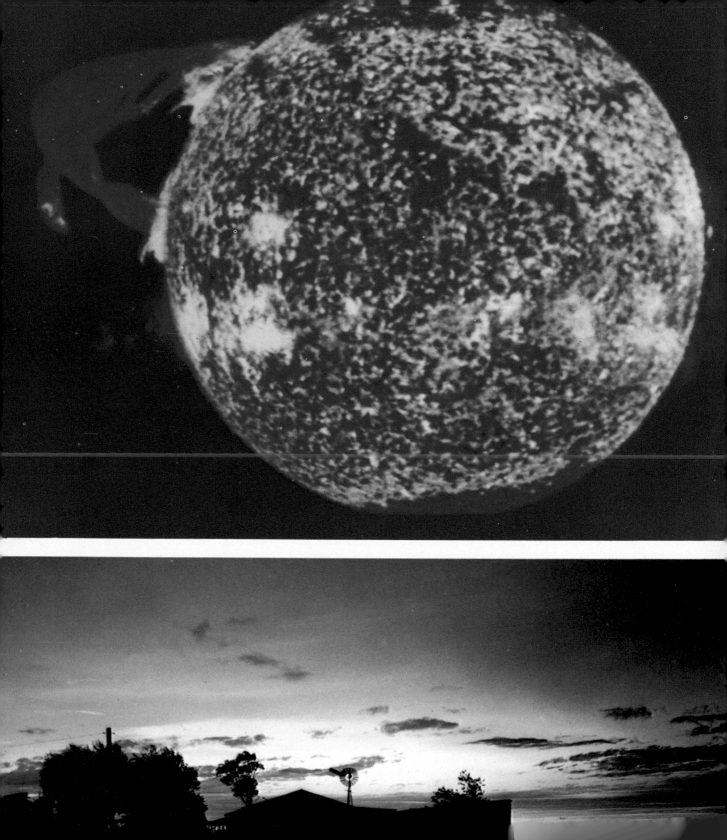

The Sun is a ball of hot gas which gives out an immense amount of energy in the form of heat and light as a result of thermo-nuclear reactions in its core; hydrogen is converted to helium under very high temperatures and pressures. Recent technological developments have resulted in an accumulation of information about the Sun which has made scientists realise that what happens in its interior is exceedingly complex. Spacecraft observations, unhampered by the Earth's atmosphere, have revealed new features of the solar surface and atmosphere. This gigantic solar flare *left* was photographed by NASA's Skylab 4 and spans 588,000 kilometres across the Sun's surface, extending many thousands of kilometres into space.

Man has recognised from earliest times the life-giving role of the Sun, and his fear when witnessing an unexpected eclipse was understandable. An eclipse of the Sun occurs when the Moon passes between it and the Earth; the Moon may obscure the Sun totally or partially, depending on the position of the observer on the Earth. From any one place on Earth a total eclipse of the Sun occurs about once in 360 years. This picture *bottom left* was taken in Melbourne, Australia, in October 1976 and shows the eerie half-light before the eclipse became total.

Right and below: Sunsets, the colours of which are explained overleaf.

Seen from space the Sun shines with an intense white light and the surrounding sky is jet black, yet on Earth the Sun looks yellow, orange or red and the sky appears blue. White light is composed of different colours, each of which represents light of a particular wavelength. As sunlight passes through the atmosphere it is scattered by the gas particles there; blue light, which has the shortest wavelength, is scattered most of all, so much so that the sky appears blue. In the evening when the Sun is low in the sky the distance the light has to travel through the atmosphere before reaching the observer is much increased, so now the yellow light is also noticeably scattered and the sun itself looks red. This explains the colour of the setting sun and the clouds in the pictures on the previous page (the colour of the Skylab photograph is due to the special photographic methods used).

When white light is bent or refracted by passing through two faces of a prism it is divided into its constituent colours. Sunlight shining through raindrops is also refracted in this way producing the colours of the rainbow *below;* spray from a large waterfall like the Victoria Falls *left* can also produce a rainbow.

Right: The midnight sun shining in summer in Greenland.

This delicate circle of light around the Sun *left* is known as a halo. It is created in the same way as a rainbow, but the light is refracted by tiny ice crystals high in the upper atmosphere and the colours are generally so mixed up that the halo appears white. The ice crystals are contained in clouds which may not always be apparent because of their high altitude. All clouds are composed of tiny water droplets or ice crystals. Cumulonimbus clouds are caused by strong ascending air currents and give rise to violent rain-storms, hail *below,* thunder-storms *bottom right* and tornadoes. Cumulus and cumulonimbus clouds have massive globular forms with great vertical height but low bases. Cirrus are high altitude clouds of a rather wispy nature, sometimes known as mares' tails. Cirrus and cumulus clouds are shown *right;* in this picture there is a mirage below the Sun. A mirage is an optical illusion created when light from an object passes through air of different temperatures, and therefore of different densities, and is refracted to make a false image. The position of a mirage depends on the relative positions of the warm and cooler layers of air; desert mirages may be inverted below the object and cold mirages may be seen the right way up above the object.

9

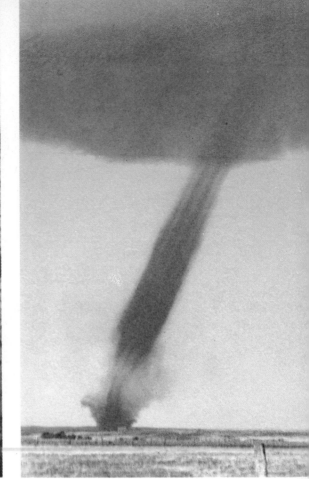

Men have observed and attempted to predict the weather from earliest times because of its importance in their lives. Weather forecasting is now more accurate than ever before, although many people feel it still leaves a lot to be desired! Weather satellites assist forecasters by taking photographs of the approaching weather systems. The picture *far left* was taken from Apollo 7 in 1968 and shows hurricane Gladys. A hurricane is a very violent tropical storm which originates as a huge spinning wind system above the sea; it covers thousands of square kilometres and has internal wind speeds of up to 240 kilometres per hour. In the western Pacific such a storm is called a typhoon and in Australia it is known as a willy-willy. Hurricanes present problems for weather forecasters because their behaviour is very erratic and it is impossible to predict the sudden changes in course that they often make. Once a hurricane has moved onto land it gradually loses intensity but it has the power to cause very great damage in coastal areas.

The tornado or twister is the most localised but most violent of all wind storms. Opinions are divided about the speed of the winds; most accept that the circulating winds often reach 400 kilometres per hour and some quote figures as high as 700 kilometres per hour. Tornadoes are most common in central North America but also occur in Australia; this one *above* was photographed in

Oklahoma in August 1965. The dark colour is typical and is due to condensed water vapour and to debris and dust picked up by the powerful ascending winds. The streaks within the vortex show an inner core, a feature of some tornadoes not often visible in photographs. The life of a tornado is short, seldom being more than an hour, but the damage it can cause is enormous. Warning services have been operating for some time in the United States and many lives have certainly been saved since their inception. Less powerful rotational winds like this minor whirlwind photographed at Bracknell, England, *bottom left* can also cause damage to property.

Tornadoes generally develop at the edge of large thunder-storms, the dark funnel appearing to descend from the cumulonimbus clouds. The mechanics of the phenomenon of lightning *right and below* are not fully understood but it appears that electrical charges are built up in the atmosphere when strong rising air currents carry water particles upwards in the cloud. The massive electrical discharge seen as a flash of lightning is accompanied by the noise of thunder caused by the expansion and contraction of the air near the discharge; this reaches the observer an appreciable amount of time after he perceives the flash, depending on his distance from it, because light travels over 800,000 times faster than sound.

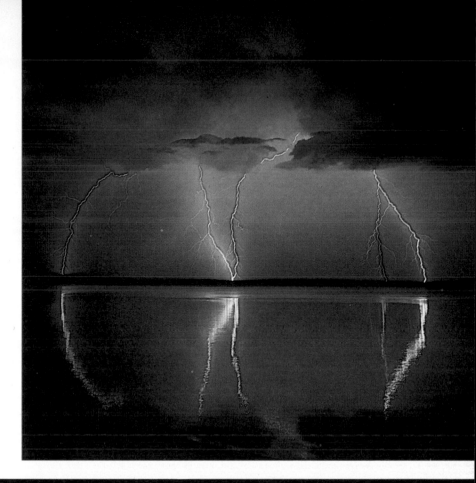

Volcanoes are shaped by relatively localised forces inside the Earth's crust and mantle but their eruptions can manifest themselves in several different ways: by violent explosions, by the formation of clouds of ash and cinder, by vast lava flows and by jets of steam, hot water or mud. The famous Krakatoa eruption of 1883 was an explosion which released enormous volumes of ash into the atmosphere and resulted in spectacular sunsets all round the world for two or three years afterwards. The dust layer caused a world-wide drop in the solar radiation reaching the Earth and has been correlated with historical records of bad summers and poor harvests. This adds weight to a suggestion first made in 1952 that volcanic eruptions could be responsible for the development of the glaciers and ice caps of the ice ages.

Volcanic activity is associated with the creation of mid-ocean ridges and with the destruction of the oceanic crust. Lavas from volcanoes at the first of these positions are composed of basalts which come from the melting of the rocks of the upper part of the mantle; the composition of the basalt is almost identical in all the oceans of the world. The lavas of volcanoes situated above ocean trenches, those in the Andes are an example, are more variable in composition; they come from three separate sources, the upper mantle, the melting of the oceanic plate itself and the lower part of the continental crust. Most of the world's volcanoes are on the so-called Ring of Fire which lies along the boundaries of the Pacific Ocean basin. All those illustrated *left* come from this ring. Augustine Island is in Alaska *top,* Cotopaxi is in Ecuador *centre* and Nguaruhoe *bottom* is in New Zealand. These three all have the pointed volcanic cones typified by Fujiyama and Vesuvius.

Kilauea Iki, shown erupting *right,* is a volcano in the Hawaiian archipelago and has the rounded flanks made by solidified lavas from slow upwellings rather than a pointed cone made from the debris ejected during violent eruptions. The fluid basalt lavas stream downhill; such lava flows have been aptly named Rivers of Fire. The basalts are very hot and fluid so volcanic gases can escape freely and the build up of pressure resulting in violent explosions does not occur. The gentle and regular Hawaiian eruptions are particularly safe and suitable for scientific study and a U.S. Federal Volcanological Observatory has been set up on Kilauea in almost ideal conditions; the weather is favourable for observations throughout the year and access is quick and convenient through Honolulu.

The severity in terms of explosiveness of a volcanic eruption depends on the nature of the magma, that is the combination of lava and volcanic gas which feeds the volcano. Rapid rise of gas through a runny lava can result in spectacular lava fountains like this one on Kilauea *right*. Photographed in the daytime, it shows the darker, cooler fragments of lava descending from the fountain.

Lavas in some eruptions are much more viscous, but it is the gas content which controls the nature of the explosion which may follow from a more or less instantaneous expansion of large volumes of gas. This boulder measuring more than one and a half metres across *left* was ejected from Poas volcano in Costa Rica and very much larger bombs have been described.

The volcanoes of the East African rift system do not appear to be associated with the creation or destruction of oceanic crust; the lavas are basaltic like the oceanic volcanoes but contain unusually high amounts of sodium and potassium. This is molten lava at night on Nyiragongo, Zaire *below*.

15

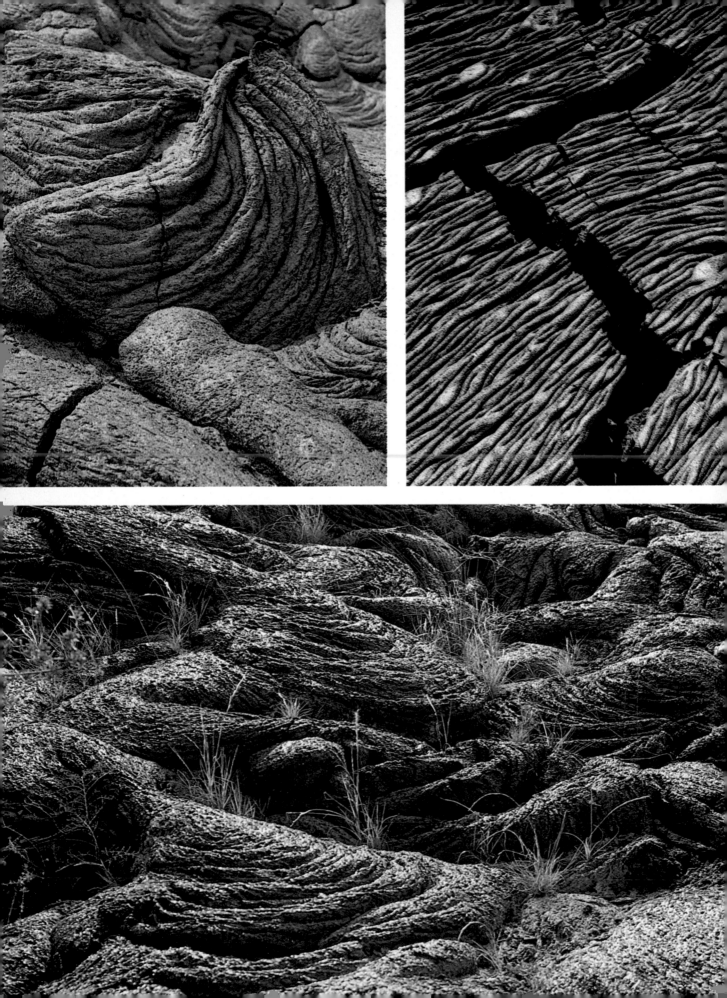

When a basalt lava flow cools, the surface takes on one of two different forms; it can be rough and rubbly or have a billowing, undulating, pleated or rope-like surface. Chemically there appears to be no difference between these forms but geologists distinguish the two types using old Hawaiian names, aa is the more common rubbly type and pahoehoe is the ropy kind. Pahoehoe flows *left* are often well-developed on oceanic volcanoes like the Hawaiian ones; these three pictures were taken in the Galapagos Islands.

The damage to human life and property from erupting volcanoes is well known and details of the classic eruption of Vesuvius in A.D. 79 have been revealed not only by contemporary accounts of the disaster but also by the remarkable preservation of Pompeii and Herculaneum by the falling ash. Ash has preserved poignant evidence of a much earlier eruption in the Acahualinca footprints *right*. These human and feline prints are 5,000–6,000 years old and were probably made by those fleeing from an eruption of Masaya volcano, Nicaragua. The mud through which the people ran was hardened and preserved by the layer of volcanic ash with which it was covered.

The Society Islands, which include Tahiti, are volcanic. The jagged peaks *below* create dramatically beautiful scenery.

18

When a thick basalt lava flow cools, a process which may take years, it shrinks and develops cracks perpendicular to the cooling surface. These develop into columns which are typically six-sided *far left* although pillars with four, five, seven or eight sides are known. Good examples of this columnar jointing can be found in Britain at the Giant's Causeway, Antrim, and at Fingal's Cave on the Isle of Staffa *below*. These thick flows must have taken years to cool – a recently measured pool of lava one hundred metres deep in Kilauea crater had a solidified crust of only six metres after seven months.

Obsidian *left* is volcanic glass formed from a magma particularly rich in silica, but free of gas, which was erupted as a partially congealed and quickly solidifying lava. It and the familiar pumice of the bathroom have identical chemical composition but pumice is formed from a magma rich in gas. Because the silica-rich lava is thick and viscous the gas bubbles have difficulty in escaping and the eruptions of the resulting froth are among the most violent known. The lava cools and solidifies during its passage through the air and the spaces that contained the gas are preserved.

Many volcanic products are, or have been, of economic importance. Pumice is not only used in bathrooms but also in the manufacture of cement and as a mild abrasive. It is sometimes used locally for the most surprising things. In the Canary Islands, for example, it is spread on fields, so protecting the soil from the hot summer sun but allowing the rain to soak straight through. In prehistoric times obsidian was in demand because it made the best and sharpest tools then available; early obsidian trade routes are traceable in Europe and Central America. Volcanic ashes are often extremely fertile, which is one reason why people return and rebuild houses on the slopes of active volcanoes; another volcanic product known as scoria is used for building aggregate. Valuable mineral deposits such as borax and sulphur are also associated with volcanoes.

When the lava in the vent of a volcano, shown red-hot in this picture of Santiago volcano, Nicaragua *top right*, cools and solidifies it is often covered by rainwater making a small crater lake. Sulphur from the volcano is sometimes dissolved in the water, creating lakes of dilute sulphuric acid like this one on Irazu volcano, Costa Rica *bottom right*.

Geysers and hot springs are manifestations of volcanic activity that man has also used to his advantage. Houses in Iceland have been heated by cheap natural steam for years but those harnessing such power in other areas have discovered that the surface displays of geysers were diminished, with a corresponding decrease in revenue from tourists. Old Faithful in Yellowstone National Park, Wyoming *left,* is one of the most famous geysers of all, not because of the height of its display, which, although considerable is topped by many others, but because of the amazing regularity of its eruptions. These used to occur at hourly intervals but recently the geyser has become more erratic and as little as thirty and as much as ninety minutes can elapse between eruptions. Old Faithful has ejected as much as 500,000 litres of water in five minutes. Thermal pools such as Doublet Pool in Yellowstone Park *below* can be very colourful, being stained by minerals and coloured by algae which flourish in the hot mineral-laden water. Non-eruptive flows of such water can lead to the production of wedding-cake terraces like these at Pamukkale in Turkey *right* where the water leaves calcium carbonate deposits as it cools.

A geyser is a hot spring from which water and steam are expelled vigorously and intermittently; well-known collections of geysers occur in New Zealand (including this one at Rotorua *left*), the United States, Iceland, the Azores, Mexico, South America and Japan. The mechanism of geyser eruption depends on the existence of a deep and narrow opening in the rock, very hot at the lower level, into which water seeps. Normal convection is prevented by the narrowness of the tube so that the water at the bottom becomes heated above normal boiling point. Eventually water in the upper part of the tube begins to boil and some of the top layer is thrown out. The release of pressure causes a rapid and progressive production of steam which leads to the explosive ejection of all the water in the tube. If the outlet channels are wide and unobstructed the heated water can escape at a relatively lower temperature and pressure, so forming the less dramatic hot spring. Most of the water which is heated in this way is rain water which has seeped down from the surface.

This mud volcano *bottom right* near Cartagena, Colombia, is an unusual product of the mixture of subterranean water with fine rock material which has resulted in a structure now about eighteen metres high.

Fumaroles are steam and gas vents which occur on volcanoes, in the lava flows, or even appear at some distance from a known volcano. They are sometimes classified according to the gases they emit, which is partly dependent on temperature. Some geysers and hot springs are technically steam fumaroles. The fumaroles on the cinder cone of Poas volcano, Costa Rica, *top right* are sulphuric fumaroles, ejecting steam and hydrogen sulphide and having the unpleasant smell of rotten eggs. Crystalline sulphur can be seen around them. There are many sulphur-rich volcanoes in the world—two in Chile are mined for their sulphur—but most of the world's sulphur comes from other sources because the low price of sulphur usually makes mining volcanoes an uneconomic proposition.

The geysers and hot springs of Yellowstone are related to fault lines. A fault is a fracture in rock along which there has been a measurable amount of displacement; the fractures occur because the rocks are under tension, often because of pressures which are exerted at plate margins. One of the most notorious faults in the world is the San Andreas fault, created by the Pacific plate sliding past the North American plate, which it is doing at a rate of about seven metres per century. If it continues at this rate Los Angeles will be alongside San Francisco in roughly eight million years.

Earthquakes occur all over the world but are especially abundant in well-defined tracts called seismic zones which, when mapped, can be seen to correspond to what are believed to be plate margins. This is a virtually identical distribution with that of volcanoes but there is no direct connection between earthquakes and volcanoes except that they have a common origin in the movement of the crustal plates. Earthquakes are related to faults, and may be caused by the sudden release of tension along a fault in the Earth's crust. Earthquake prediction and possible control is a growing science but there are enormous problems, financial and political as well as scientific. This collapsed road *left* is the result of an earthquake in Guatemala.

The East African rift system, of which Olduvai Gorge in Tanzania *below* is a part, can be traced for thousands of kilometres through Africa and into the Red Sea. A rift valley, this gorge is an example, is formed by roughly parallel faults which have caused the land between them to drop relative to the land on either side. The rifting, together with the basaltic composition of the volcanoes in the area, has suggested the intriguing possibility that the continent is destined to split along the rifts, so this could be a new ocean in the making.

The Andes *right,* Himalayas *far right* and the Alps *below* are among the best known mountain ranges in the world. The Andes, as we have already seen, are the result of a collision between an oceanic plate and the South American plate. The heat generated by the oceanic plate passing under the continental one has resulted in a huge mass of molten granite being injected into this volcanic mountain range. This picture of the northernmost section of the Andes gives some idea of the immense forces acting laterally and resulting in the massive and regular folds of the mountains.

The Himalayas have been created by a collision which started as recently as sixty-five million years ago and which probably still continues between the two continental plates of India and Eurasia. The crustal upheavals have lifted thick layers of marine-deposited rocks from a deep ocean trench so that marine fossils can be found high up in the mountains. Mountain ranges consist of intensely deformed rocks; the Alps are no exception and are particularly remarkable for their complex history and structure.

25

Geologists distinguish three main types of rock, igneous, metamorphic and sedimentary. Igneous rocks include the basalts and granites already mentioned; metamorphic rocks are those which have been changed by heat and pressure from their original state; sedimentary rocks, of which about three-quarters of the exposed rocks on this planet are composed, are created at or near the surface by entirely different processes. There are two main sources of material from which sedimentary rocks are made: inorganic rock materials removed by erosion, and organic remains or products from plants and animals. Most are deposited as sediments in calm parts of rivers, lakes and seas; these sediments are turned into rocks by cementation and compaction.

One characteristic feature of sedimentary rocks is layering, bedding or stratification, which stems from variations in the conditions under which the rocks were laid down. Differences in the volume or velocity of a river or the depth of an ocean will lead to differences in the size of rock debris being deposited in any particular place and to differences in its composition. On some parts of the sea coast large particles will be transported and deposited, whereas in shallow calm waters the particles will be tiny. If the sea encroaches on the land the deposits will be different again – coal seams are the results of such marine invasion. The successive beds laid down in, say, a marine environment are normally horizontal; subsequent earth movements frequently alter this configuration.

Sedimentary rocks forming the Grand Canyon *top left* still remain horizontal despite their uplift and show clear parallel strata. Twelve major layers can easily be distinguished by the visitor to the Canyon. This area is now being heavily eroded and it has been calculated that the Colorado River is washing one million tons of mud, sand and gravel downstream every day. This material will be incorporated into the sedimentary rocks of the future.

The Bahama Banks are made up of calcareous deposits which have formed a large submarine plateau two or three kilometres high during the last 150 million years. The area is isolated from land-formed sediments so the sand on beaches in the area *bottom left* is very pale, almost pure white.

Besides their horizontal layering, sedimentary rocks have many other features by which they may be recognised; these include ripple marks. The ripple marks *top right* were made by the sea on an existing beach in Nova Scotia, those *centre* are from the Moenkopi formation at Capitol Reef National Monument, Utah, and were left more than 200 million years ago by the waters on a receding shoreline. The ripples *bottom right* are also "fossilised" and were photographed in Greenland.

Sedimentary rocks can reveal a great deal about the geological history of an area. The rocks *below* are clearly bent up to form a shallow arch, known as an anticline; this is at Hartland Quay, Devon, England. Not far away at Millook Haven in Cornwall the rocks of the Crackington formation have been folded in a much more complicated fashion *right*. The Organ Pipes *far left* have been exposed by the Finke River in the Macdonnell Ranges of Central Australia and what were once horizontal strata on a sea bed are now vertical. They were almost certainly part of a large anticline, the other side of which is either buried or already eroded. The zigzag folds of the Crackington formation show how sedimentary layers can be turned upside down by intense folding.

The lush Guyanan rain forest with the Mazaruni River running through it *left* does not look geologically revealing but it is probable that this river is running along a fault line–the straight channel certainly suggests some underlying feature governing its course.

Wind and water are obvious examples of agents of erosion but glaciers too make a major contribution. Ten per cent of the land area of the Earth is ice-covered today, but during the last two million years there have been repeated episodes during which about thirty per cent of the land area was glaciated.

Left: The massive glacier in the Western Cwm of Everest.
Right: The north wall of the Grandes Jorasses in the French Alps showing a main glacier, subsidiary glacier, cwms and arrêts.
Below: The snout of Nordenskold Glacier, South Georgia, with the leading edge deformed into weird shapes by repeated freezing and thawing.

Glaciers form wherever winter snowfall regularly exceeds summer melt. They form the ice sheets of Greenland and Antarctica and valley glaciers in mountain ranges elsewhere; the altitude of the permanent snow line is largely dependent on the latitude. Successive layers of fallen snow become more and more compacted until solid ice is formed. Because of the thickness and pressure, the ice can move or flow; this solid mass of slowly moving ice is a glacier. Glaciers carry a large amount of material both on and underneath them in the form of rock fragments ranging from boulders which fall from the valley sides to finest rock flour which has been ground from the underlying rock by the passage of the glacier. Such rock material can be seen in this picture *left* of the lower part of a glacier beneath the Chamonix Aiguilles in the French Alps. This material is deposited by the glacier at its end as the ice melts; these rock deposits are known as a moraine.

Nearly all icebergs are formed as the ice sheets of Greenland and Antarctica flow out over the sea and break under their own weight. Greenland icebergs can extend 100 metres or so above the water and weigh one million tons; those in Antarctica are flatter and much longer reaching up to 160 kilometres in length. Portage Glacier in Alaska is a valley glacier *below* which "calves" small icebergs in the same way, in this case into the waters of Portage Lake.

Right: Annapurna Glacier.

"calves" small icebergs in the same way, in this case into the waters of Portage Lake.
Many valley glaciers have tributaries which join the main glacier. These tributary valleys are not deepened by the ice as much as the larger main valley so when the ice retreats the small valleys can be seen to join high up on the side of the main trough. A hanging valley in Greenland is shown on the right hand side of the picture *left*. A glacial valley is typically U-shaped and at the head there is usually a nearly circular basin with steep sides which is known as a corrie, cirque or cwm. The picture of a glacier on Mount Patterson in the Canadian Rockies *below* shows the cwm clearly; there is frost-shattered scree and glacier-pulverised rock in the foreground. A cwm originates as a hollow containing a patch of snow and ice which gradually enlarges until it over-flows. As the ice moves it erodes the sides and bottom of the cwm, steepening the sides and deepening the original hollow.

Top right: An iceberg in the Antarctic.
Below: The terminal moraine of an old glacier in the Columbia Icefield in Alberta.

Glaciers cause erosion in two principal ways. One is by plucking out loose fragments of rock from their bed and dragging them along, the other is by abrasion—the rock fragments already in the ice grind and scour at the underlying rock. This results in scoring and scratching of the rock making striations which run parallel to the direction of flow of the glacier or ice sheet. The scarred rock at the front of the Moreno Glacier in Argentina *left* and in Greenland *below* illustrate the force of glacial erosion.

The depositional effect of glaciers can be seen in those lowland areas which were modified by glaciers during the Ice Ages; the ice sheets deposited vast quantities of morainic material and the masses of water released from the melting ice further shaped the landscape into gently undulating areas of mainly fertile soils with patches of poor drainage as in Ontario, Canada *right*.

Erosion caused by water running in a stream or river is not unlike that achieved by a glacier. A river carries small particles of rock and soil in suspension, rolling larger pieces of rock along the bed and wearing this and the banks away in the process. Waterfalls originate because of different rates of erosion on different types of bedrock. If a river passes from a layer of resistant rock onto much softer rock the latter will erode more quickly and a distinct step or small waterfall will appear. The falling water will excavate the bed at its base even further. Iguazu Falls on the borders of Argentina and Brazil *left* and Niagara Falls on the borders of Canada and the United States, here seen from an aeroplane *below,* are two of the biggest waterfalls in the continent of America. Waterfalls continually erode themselves; the Niagara Falls are retreating upriver at a rate of between one and two metres a year. The rock in the centre of Niagara's Horseshoe Falls is softer than that at the edge and is eroded more quickly making the horseshoe shape. Waterfalls are also formed from hanging valleys.

Right: Delicate falls in the volcanic rocks at Takachiho, Japan.

40

When rain falls onto the earth it is distributed in various ways. Some evaporates back into the atmosphere, some soaks into the ground; there is a level of impermeability below which it cannot penetrate and water seeping down to this level gradually saturates the rocks above. The upper level of this saturated zone is known as the water table; this fluctuates according to rainfall and in some places it reaches the surface in the form of springs. Water flowing to the sea over the face of the land is the dominant agent of landscape alteration. As a river cuts into the sides of its valley these are exposed to weathering and this, together with the river's undercutting action of its banks, causes further collapse typically resulting in a V-shaped valley. In arid areas, where there is little erosion of the valley sides, narrow, steep-sided gorges form; the Grand Canyon is such a gorge. From the Toroweap Overlook *near left* the sides drop vertically for 1,000 metres to the Colorado River below. Gorges also form in very hard rock which is resistant to weathering and in very permeable rock where the rainwater soaks quickly into the ground and does not erode the surface.

Individual river systems vary, but in general the upper reaches are steep and narrow with rapid water flow, while wide meanders with slow-moving water are typical of a river near its mouth. The underlying rocks will control the course of the river in its upper reaches. Rain falling on the Sierra Nevada de Santa Marta in Colombia, the northernmost part of the Andes, runs off the ridges in streams which run into a larger stream flowing at right angles to them in a natural valley in the folded rocks *right.*

It is a little understood but basic property of water to flow in curving arcs and this is believed to be why meanders form. The water in a river then flows more rapidly on the outside edge of the bends it has made, undercutting the banks, and slower flow on the inside results in the deposition of sediment. In this way the curvature is increased, finally resulting in meanders being cut off from the main stream so forming ox-bow lakes. A meandering tributary of a river on the border between Guyana and Brazil is shown *bottom left;* the central meander looks as though it will shortly become an ox-bow lake. Sand banks of deposited material are shown in the same river *top far left.*

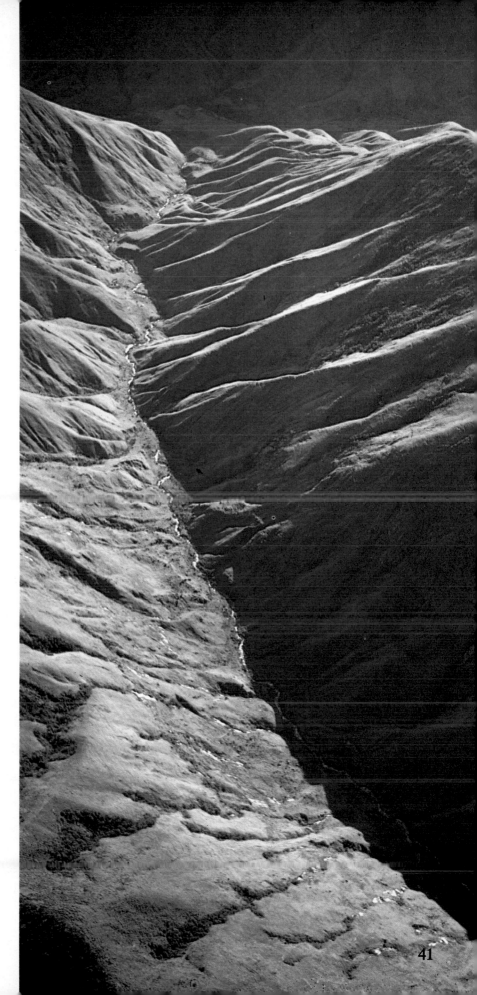

41

Underground caves are usually formed in limestone. Limestone is resistant to erosion largely because of its permeability to water which therefore tends to soak underground; in addition it is often jointed and fissured which allows the water to seep down freely. The sort of limestone in which caves occur is compact with sections composed of more easily dissolved rocks; as a result erosion occurs in the soluble rocks and so creates caves. The water which drips through the roofs of these caves has dissolved calcium carbonate in it which is readily deposited either on the ceiling or on the floor, forming stalactites and stalagmites. This deposition is usually attributed to the evaporation of water but cave air is very humid and evaporation can only be slight. Some of the deposit is caused because the dripping water is subjected to a lower pressure than that in the rocks from which it has seeped, carbon dioxide is therefore released from solution causing precipitation of calcium carbonate which forms calcite deposits called flowstone, dripstone or travertine. Undisturbed by wind and weather delicate formations are built up over thousands of years. These stalactites and stalagmites are at Cheddar, England *left*, Kango Caves near Oudtshoorn in South Africa *right* and Carlsbad Caverns, New Mexico *below*.

There are three main movements of the sea: tides, currents and waves. Tides are caused by the gravitational pull of the Sun and the Moon. The Moon, being very much nearer than the Sun, exerts the greater influence. Extra high tides (spring tides) occur when the Moon and Sun are lined up and are acting together. The lowest or neap tides occur when the gravitational attractions of the Sun and the Moon are acting at right angles to each other.

Solar energy is responsible for the ocean currents and for the atmospheric currents, or winds. Ocean currents have a profound effect on climate, cooling the coast of West Africa, Peru and the western United States and warming up Britain which would probably otherwise be under a sheet of ice.

Winds generate waves whose height depends on the strength of the wind and the extent of open water, known as the fetch, across which the wind can work. The greater the fetch the larger the waves. Huge waves are shown crashing onto a promontory in Hawaii *below;* in Waimea Bay, also in Hawaii, smaller waves break on the beach *left.* The erosional work of the sea is often rapid and spectacular. Waves have undermined this limestone cliff in the Trobriand Islands, New Guinea *right* and the mass of rock above will eventually crash into the sea.

Beaches are built up of material which comes mainly from the land and which is pounded by the sea so making rounded cobbles, pebbles, shingle, sand and mud. Sand can be made of shells like this *far left* on the Isle of Mull; the sand on Kauai, Hawaii *left*, is composed of pulverised lava, shells and coral. The large pebbles lapped by waves in southern England are mainly chalk, sandstone and flint *bottom left* while cobbles of granite, gneiss and feldspar can be found on beaches in northern Scotland *right*. The beach pebbles *below* are almost entirely quartz.

The Kauai sands illustrated are known as the Barking Sands because a strange sound rather like the barking of a dog is often produced when people walk on them. There are other sands, both beach and desert, which produce odd noises such as whistling, singing and booming. This seems to occur when the sand grains are both highly polished and of uniform size; the grains are easily displaced, and continuous vibrations are thus set up.

When waves advance obliquely on a shore line the rushing water driven up the beach as the waves break, known as the swash, will also advance obliquely, so particles on the beach will have a net movement along it. This shifting of beach material along a coast is called longshore drift. The sea also grades or sorts the pebbles, the biggest being carried to the

47

top of the beach because the swash is more powerful than the backwash. Chesil Beach is an unusual shingle ridge off the coast of Dorset in southern England; the pebbles are graded along the bank with striking precision, those at the western end being small *far right* and those at the eastern end are large *right*. Longshore drifting is obviously partly responsible for this but how the sorting occurs is not clear.

Tidal bores like those in the Maccan River which flows into the Bay of Fundy *left* and on the River Severn *below* are the result of the contact of the river current with that of the rising tide running into a funnel-shaped estuary. The tide rises faster than it can pass obstructions in the river mouth which delay the flow; eventually the sea breaks over them and a wave with a steep high front comes rolling upstream.

Bottom right: Calm sea in the English Channel at sunset.

Wind is important as an agent of erosion and transportation in deserts and other dry places. The huge mushroom-shaped rocks of The Enchanted City near Cuenca in Spain *top left* have been sand-blasted by the wind, which, because it only lifts the sand a short distance above the ground, causes most erosion at or near ground level. Wave Rock in Western Australia *bottom left* is a granite wall which has also been polished by blown sand, but weathering by water has probably been an important factor too. The sandstone of Arches National Monument, Utah, has been subjected to weathering by acidic rain-water as well as to sand-blasting by the wind resulting in the formation of huge arches like Delicate Arch *right* and Double Arch *below;* human figures show the enormous size of these arches.

Rain is largely responsible for the unusual erosion features in Turkey illustrated *overleaf left and centre.* Here thick deposits of volcanic ashes are overlain by fissured and weathered lavas. Heavy spring rains have eroded the ashes except where covered by a resistant cap of lava which has resulted in these peculiar pillars. Similar erosion occurs of the glacial deposits known as boulder clay; the resulting columns with their protective boulders perched on top are known as demoiselles or hoodoos.

A desert does not necessarily consist of vast seas of insufferably hot sand. There are cold deserts as well as hot ones and sand is not necessary for a place to be a desert–less than one sixth of the Sahara is covered with sand. A desert may be defined as an area which receives less than twenty-five centimetres of rain per year, but other factors such as temperature have to be taken into account. Nevertheless, sand dunes, a characteristic feature of wind erosion, are typical desert formations. A variety of sand forms exist, ranging from ripples *bottom right* to large dunes *top right*, here shown in the Algerian Sahara looking towards El Oued. A continuous wind sorts loose sand into ripples at right angles to the direction in which it is blowing; they look very like the ripples made by the sea on a beach. Sand dunes are born when the blown sand reaches an obstruction such as a hollow or a boulder and begins to accumulate. As the dune gets bigger sand is blown up the windward side which has quite a shallow gradient and some goes over the top, slips down and comes to rest on the other, steeper side. This results in a net movement of the dune at a rate of between ten and fifty metres per year.

A dust devil *top left* is a rotational wind which carries sand and debris with it. Large dust storms also occur in deserts; the wind can lift the dust up to heights of 3,000 metres or more, carrying fine material considerable distances. Sand from the Sahara has been brought down with rain in Spain, France and Italy. Wind-blown sand can be derived from erosion of sandstone such as that in this dry river gorge in southern Tunisia *previous page, top right* or from erosion like this in Uganda *previous page, bottom right*. This last picture shows the watercourses which carry away the fertile soil which is unprotected by vegetation; such unprotected soil is also vulnerable to wind erosion.

A curious phenomenon has been observed at the Great Salt Lake in Utah and at other normally dry lake beds in California and Nevada. Stones ranging from those the size of an orange to monsters weighing more than one third of a ton have been found resting at the end of tracks a hundred metres or more long. This example was photographed at the Great Salt Lake *bottom left*. No one had actually seen one of these stones move; the tracks were found after stormy moonless nights and all manner of agencies were invoked to explain their movement. One seriously considered possibility was that moving ice was involved, but recent research has shown that the stones are moved by high winds blowing over a surface lubricated by a thin layer of water-saturated mud.

White Sands National Monument in New Mexico *below* is a desert of pure gypsum, the largest surface deposit of its kind; it is a tourist attraction but has also been used as a rocket proving ground. The sand is soft and rubs to powder in the fingers; it too is blown into dunes by the wind.

Barren desert-like conditions may be created as mobile dunes gradually engulf oases and farmland. This can be part of a chain reaction, for desert creeps into steppe, steppe encroaches on savannah and savannah begins to invade forested areas. Man's mismanagement of the semi-arid zone is an important factor in desertification. He is guilty of overgrazing, collection of wood for fuel and of clearing sloping land for cultivation. These activities expose the precious topsoil, thus unprotected, to erosion by wind and water. Flash floods cause devastating damage, and, as the desert advances the water table falls making wells dry and agriculture no longer possible. Drought will always lead to desert conditions in the end; in Victoria, Australia *top right*, drought has increased the proportion of salts in the water of streams and these excess salts are killing the vegetation.

Left: Dunes and grasses after rain, Namibia.

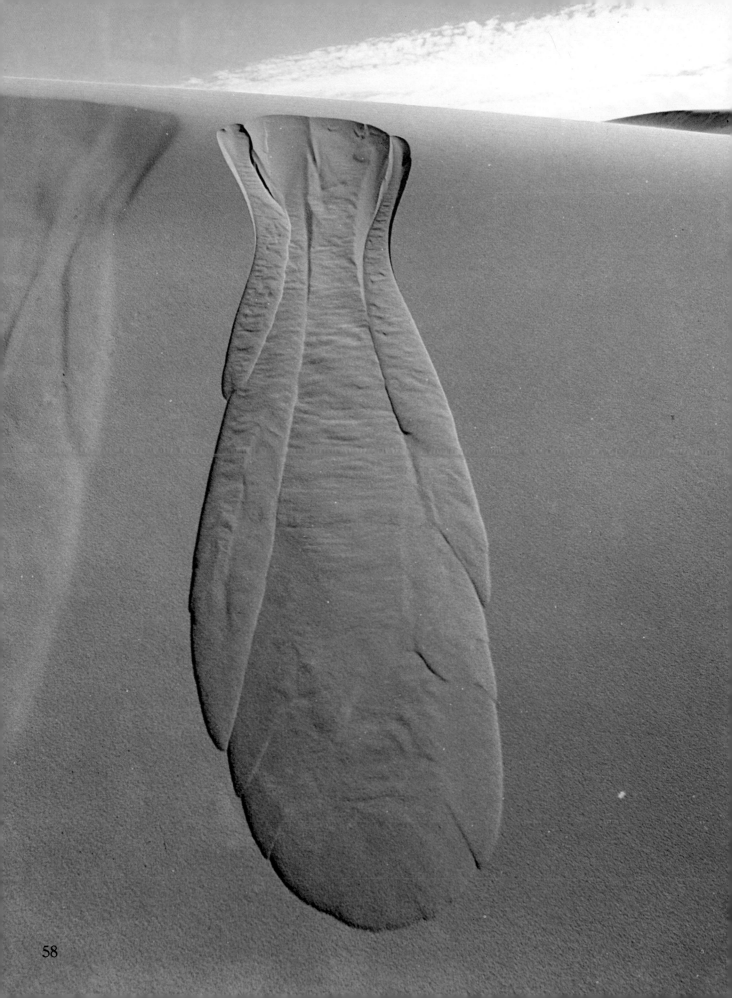

58

When rock material moves downhill under the influence of gravity but without being transported by flowing water or moving ice the results can be spectacular landslides or avalanches. The existence of clay soils can sometimes lead to dangerous earthflows like those common in the St. Lawrence valley and in parts of Norway. The water-saturated clay is stable unless disturbed by a shock such as an explosion or earthquake; then the mass spontaneously liquefies forming huge earthflows. The earthquake at Anchorage, Alaska, on 27 March 1964 triggered enormous landslides of this sort which caused more damage than the actual earthquake.

An avalanche is the most rapid and the most terrifying variety of flowing mass-movement. In composition it can vary from almost pure snow to almost entirely rock with gradations in between of varying proportions of snow, ice and rock. Avalanches are common in high mountains everywhere; these are both in the Himalayas–off the face of Nuptse *right* and off the slopes of Hium Chuli *below*, just above the area used as base camp by climbers attempting the ascent of Annapurna. If composed of loose new snow, avalanches can reach speeds of more than 300 kilometres per hour and are preceded by a shock wave which has been likened to the blast of a bomb in its effects.

Left: Sliding sand in the Namib Desert.

Water is by far and away the most abundant material on and near the surface of the Earth. It is easily taken for granted yet it has some very peculiar properties. It is the only substance which occurs naturally on the Earth in gaseous, liquid and solid states. It acts as a solvent for many different substances and is instrumental in a wide range of erosional processes. When it freezes in the cracks of rocks substantial forces are generated which force them apart. Frost can also make very beautiful patterns, like those sometimes found on window panes or these frost feathers on a pond in Alaska *left*. The delicate shapes of snow flakes *far left and below* are the skeletons of incomplete ice crystals. They are formed in clouds when crystallisation occurs slowly in calm air at a low temperature. The crystals are always six-sided with a regular geometric form but can have thousands of different shapes. By melting slightly and then refreezing they form small granules of ice which gives old snow the texture of very coarse sand. The peaceful pictures here and on the next page give little clue of the immense power of water in its various forms.

Very thin sections of rock can be cut using a special cutting machine; these can be mounted on microscope slides and viewed using polarised light. The results

Top right: Icicles dripping water during the spring break-up on Credit River, Ontario.
Bottom right: Snow on rocks in a creek in Wyoming.

are often beautifully coloured *right;* the colours are not the actual colours of the rock (the sections used are so thin that they are often virtually colourless) but are a result of using cross-polarised light. This picture shows that the rock has been deformed and the deformation of the crystals resembles that, on a different scale, of the exposed rocks of the Crackington formation, already illustrated. This was originally a sedimentary rock which has been subjected to heat and pressure resulting in the formation of a so-called metamorphic rock. (It is in fact a staurolite schist from the Dalradian formation in Scotland.)

Our understanding of the way glaciers flow comes partly from knowledge of the behaviour of ice crystals under pressure; similarly our understanding of rocks and the way they behave is helped by knowledge of crystallography. Information about geomorphological and environmental processes is accumulating rapidly; these advances are a result of increased technological sophistication coupled with a desire for knowledge which stems in part from the awareness that man has the ability to cause irreversible damage to his environment.

Left: Crystals of hoar frost on a twig.
Below: Dew drops on a spider's web.

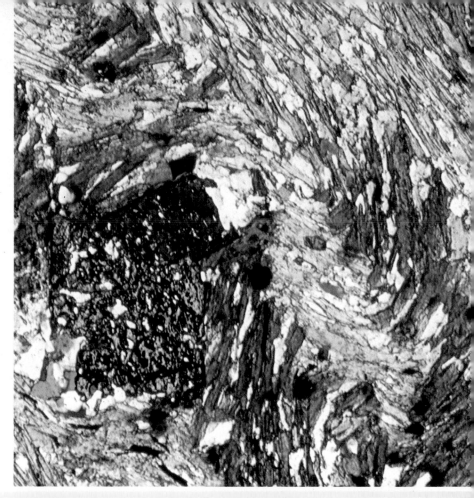

INDEX

Page numbers refer to illustrations.

Acahualinca footprints, Nicaragua	17	Kango Caves, South Africa	43
Alps	25, 31, 32	Kilauea Iki, Hawaii	13, 15
Andes	12, 25, 41	Lava	13, 14, 15, 16
Annapurna, Mt., Himalayas	33, 59	Lightning	11
Arches National Monument, Utah	51	Maccan River, Nova Scotia	48
Augustine Island, Alaska	12	Mazaruni River, Guyana	28
Avalanches	59	Mirage	9
Bahamian Sea	26	Moenkopi formation, Utah	27
Barking Sands, Kauia, Hawaii	46	Moreno Glacier, Argentina	36
Basalt (see also Lava)	18	Mud volcano, Colombia	23
Bores	48	Namib Desert, Namibia	56, 58
Cappadocia, Turkey	52	Ngauruhoe volcano, New Zealand	12
Carlsbad Caverns, New Mexico	43	Niagara Falls, Canada/United States	38
Chamonix Aiguilles, Alps	32	Nordenskold Glacier, South Georgia	31
Cheddar Caves, England	42	Nuptse, Mt., Himalayas	59
Chesil Beach, England	49	Nyiragongo volcano, Zaire	14
Clouds	5, 8, 9, 10	Obsidian	18
Colorado River, Arizona	26, 40	Old Faithful, Yellowstone, Wyoming	20
Columbia Ice Field, Alberta	35	Olduvai Gorge, Tanzania	24
Cotopaxi volcano, Ecuador	12	Organ Pipes, Central Australia	28
Crackington formation, England	29	Pamukkale, Turkey	21
Deserts	53, 55, 56, 57, 58	Patterson, Mt., Alberta	34
Dew	63	Pebbles	46, 47, 49
Doublet Pool, Yellowstone, Wyoming	20	Poas volcano, Costa Rica	14, 23
Drought	57	Portage Glacier, Alaska	32
Dust devil	54	Rainbows	6
Earth	2	Rift Valley	24
Earthquake	24	Ripples	27, 55
Eclipse	4	Rivers	26, 28, 40, 41, 48
Enchanted City, Spain	50	Rock, thin section	63
Erosion	26, 35, 38, 40, 45, 50, 51, 52, 53	Rotorua, New Zealand	22
		Sahara Desert	55
Everest, Mt., Himalayas	30	Sand	46, 47, 55, 56, 57, 58
Faulting	28		
Fingal's Cave, Staffa, Scotland	18	Santiago volcano, Nicaragua	19
Folding	25, 28, 29, 41, 63	Sea	26, 44, 45, 49
Frost	60, 62	Severn, River, England	48
Fumaroles	23	Sierra Nevada de Santa Marta, Colombia	25, 41
Fundy, Bay of, Nova Scotia	48	Snow	60, 61
Geysers	20, 22	Solar flare	4
Glaciers	30, 31, 32, 33, 34, 35, 36, 37	Springs, hot	20, 21
		Stalactites and stalagmites	42, 43
Grand Canyon, Arizona	26, 40	Sun	4, 5, 7, 8
Grandes Jorasses, Alps	31	Tahiti	17
Great Salt Lake, Utah	54	Takachiho Falls, Japan	39
Greenland	7, 27, 34, 37	Thunder-clouds	9
Gypsum	57	Tornado	10
Hail	8	Trobriand Islands, New Guinea	45
Halo	8	Victoria Falls, Zambia/Rhodesia	6
Hawaii	13, 15, 44, 45, 46	Volcanoes	6, 12, 13, 14, 15, 19, 23
Himalayas	25, 30, 33, 59		
Hium Chuli, Mt., Himalayas	59	Waterfalls	6, 38, 39
Hurricane	10	Wave Rock, Western Australia	50
Icebergs	32, 35	Waves	44, 45
Icicles	61	Whirlwind	10
Iguazu Falls, Brazil/Argentina	38	White Sands National Monument, New Mexico	57
Irazu volcano, Costa Rica	19		

First published in Great Britain 1978 by Colour Library International Ltd.
© Text: Jacqueline Seymour. © Illustrations: CLI/Bruce Coleman Ltd.
Colour separations by La Cromolito, Milan, Italy. Printed and bound by L.E.G.O., Vicenza, Italy.
Display and text filmsetting by Focus Photoset, London, England.
Published by Crescent Books, a division of Crown Publishers Inc.
All rights reserved. Library of Congress Catalogue Card No. 78-50648
CRESCENT 1978